DOGS HELPING PEOPLE

Detector Dogs

Sniffing Out Trouble

Alice B. McGinty

The Rosen Publishing Group's
PowerKids Press ™
New York

Published in 1999 by The Rosen Publishing Group, Inc.
29 East 21st Street, New York, NY 10010

First Edition

Book Design: Michael de Guzman

Photo Credits: p. 4 © Charlie Palek/Animals Animals; p. 7 © Bill Silliker Jr./Animals Animals; pp. 8,15 © Ron Chapple/FPG International; p. 11 © Jerry Cooke/Animals Animals; p. 12 © Norvia Behling/Animals Animals; p. 16 © Mark Reinstein/FPG International; p.19 © Lee Foster/FPG International; p. 20 © Henry Ausloos/Animals Animals.

McGinty, Alice B. (Alice Blumenthal)
    Detector dogs: sniffing out trouble / by Alice B. McGinty.
        p.   cm. — (Dogs helping people)
    Includes index.
    Summary: Discusses what a detector dog is, the training it goes through, different
    kinds of search dogs, and their jobs.
    ISBN 0-8239-5217-7
    1. Police dogs—Juvenile literature. 2. Search dogs—Juvenile literature. [1. Police dogs.
    2. Search dogs. 3. Dogs.] I. Title. II. Series: McGinty, Alice B. Dogs helping people.
HV8025.M33   1998
363.232—dc21   97-53114
                                              CIP
                                              AC

Manufactured in the United States of America

Contents

Ready's Rag

Ready is a bouncy **golden retriever** (GOL-den ree-TREE-ver). One day a visitor comes to the animal shelter where Ready lives. The visitor gives Ready a rolled-up rag. They play tug-of-war. Then they play fetch. Ready loves to play!

"Ready would make a fine detector dog," the visitor says. "She is **alert** (uh-LERT), smart, and friendly." The visitor adopts Ready. "You'll play with this rag again, Ready," says the visitor. "It is going to help you become a detector dog!"

◀ *Dogs chosen to be detector dogs should be healthy, well-mannered, and at least one year old.*

Detector Dogs

Detector dogs help people find things. They are like detectives who look for clues. There are many kinds of detector dogs. Each kind searches for different types of clues.

When detector dogs search, they don't search with their eyes. They follow their noses! Dogs have super noses. They can smell things that people can't. Dogs sniff everything around them. They live in a world of smells.

The police, the **military** (MIH-lih-ter-ee), and the United States **government** (GUH-vern-ment) all use detector dogs to help them.

The Labrador retriever is one kind of dog that is used as a detector dog. ▶

Narcotics-Detector Dogs

Narcotics (nar-KAH-tiks) are **illegal** (il-LEE-gul) drugs. Many detector dogs become narcotics-detector dogs. Narcotics-detector dogs help police officers find illegal drugs. Then the drugs can be thrown away and their owner can be arrested.

Some people sell narcotics to make money. The police work to stop them. **Customs** (KUS-tumz) is a part of the government that works to stop them too. Ready will go to training school to become a narcotics-detector dog.

Customs uses narcotics-detector dogs to help them sniff out drugs in people's bags at airports.

Training School

In narcotics-detector training school a dog and her **handler** (HAND-ler) play fetch with a rag. After a while the handler puts narcotics in the rag.

After more fetch, they play hide-and-seek. "Find it," the handler says. The dog uses her nose to search for the hidden rag. She finds it. "Good dog," says her handler.

Next, narcotics are hidden without the rag. The dog is now used to searching for the smell of narcotics. She finds it. The handler tosses the rag to the dog, and they play.

For a detector dog in training, playtime is also a time for learning. ▷

Learning the Tricks

Now the trainer hides narcotics in strange places. The dog finds narcotics hidden under floors, in cars, and even in toilets. People hide illegal drugs in many strange places. A detector dog has to be ready to look everywhere!

People try to cover the smell of narcotics with other strong smells. A detector dog learns to find narcotics hidden in perfume bottles, under onions, and in boxes of coffee.

◀ *A detector dog's training takes place both indoors and outdoors.*

On the Job

The dog and her handler have finished their training. Now they work with the Customs Department. Customs stops people from **smuggling** (SMUH-gling), or sneaking, narcotics and other illegal things into the United States.

The dog sniffs luggage arriving at an airport. She stops at one suitcase and scratches it. This is called **alerting** (uh-LER-ting). The dog is saying that she smells narcotics. Customs officers search the suitcase. A big bag of narcotics is found inside. "Good dog," the handler says.

A detector dog will scratch and even bark ▶
at a suitcase when she is alerting.

Bomb-Detector Dogs

In another airport, workers get a call: "There's a bomb on Flight 409." Passengers quickly leave the plane. Then workers bring in a bomb-detector dog. He has been trained to search for **explosives** (ek-SPLOH-sivz). Explosives are what make bombs explode.

The dog sniffs everywhere. Suddenly he stops. He stares hard at a box on the luggage rack. Bomb-detector dogs alert by staring or barking. They never scratch at a bomb!

Workers carefully remove the bomb. The dog has saved the plane and many lives.

◀ *Bomb-detector dogs also work with police to find explosives in cars.*

17

Accelerant-Detector Dogs

An **arsonist** (AR-sun-ist) pours gasoline inside a building and sets it on fire. Gasoline is an **accelerant** (ek-SEL-er-ent). It makes fire spread quickly. Soon the building has burned down.

Later, firefighters search what's left after the fire. Another helper comes too: an accelerant-detector dog. She searches for accelerants like gasoline. The dog sniffs the **rubble** (RUH-bul). She points her nose to a spot on the floor. It's gasoline! Now firefighters know that the fire was started on purpose. Police will look for the person who started the fire. That person will go to jail.

Accelerant-detector dogs work in an area such as this one, which has ▶ been destroyed by fire.

18

Body-Detector Dogs

Sometimes fires, floods, earthquakes, and other **disasters** (dih-ZAS-terz) hurt people. Body-detector dogs are trained to find people who are trapped under heavy buildings or other **debris** (duh-BREE) that may have fallen during a disaster.

Body-detector dogs are trained in the same way as other detector dogs. Trainers cover the dog's toy with something that smells like a person. Then the dogs practice searching for that smell in many different places. Some police dogs are trained to be body-detector dogs. Then they can help the police on searches.

◀ *A body-detector dog's sharp sense of smell can lead police to a pond or lake where someone may need help.*

21

Those Super Noses

Detector dogs, like Ready, enjoy using their trained noses to find things. And people are glad they do. Narcotics-detector dogs find large amounts of illegal drugs. Bomb-detector dogs work faster than people and find bombs minutes before they explode. Accelerant-detector dogs help firefighters learn the cause of a fire. And body-detector dogs find people who are stuck under collapsed buildings. Detector dogs can help people in many ways!

Glossary

accelerant (ek-SEL-er-ent) Something that makes a fire start and spread quickly.

alert (uh-LERT) Knowing what is going on around you.

alerting (uh-LER-ting) Signaling.

arsonist (AR-sun-ist) A person who starts a fire on purpose.

Customs (KUS-tumz) A part of the government that works to stop the smuggling of illegal drugs or other goods.

debris (duh-BREE) What is left after something has been destroyed.

disaster (dih-ZAS-ter) Something bad that happens.

explosive (ek-SPLOH-siv) Something that can explode.

golden retriever (GOL-den ree-TREE-ver) A kind of dog with long yellow or gold hair that weighs between 60 and 75 pounds.

government (GUH-vern-ment) The people who run a state or country.

handler (HAND-ler) The person who works with a detector dog, such as a police officer.

illegal (il-LEE-gul) Against the law.

military (MIH-lih-ter-ee) Part of the government that protects the United States.

narcotics (nar-KAH-tiks) Illegal drugs.

rubble (RUH-bul) Broken parts of a building and other things left after the building has burned down.

smuggling (SMUH-gling) Sneaking something into or out of a country.

Index